T0054500

the correct fury of your why is a mountain

kevin andrew heslop

GORDON HILL
PRESS

Edited by Shane Neilson
Cover and book design by Jeremy Luke Hill
Proofreading by Carol Dilworth
Set in Mrs. Eaves and Futura
Printed on Mohawk Via Felt
Printed and bound by Arkay Design & Print

LIBRARY AND ARCHIVES CANADA CATALOGUING IN PUBLICATION

Title: The correct fury of your why is a mountain / Kevin Andrew Heslop.
Names: Heslop, Kevin, 1992- author.
Description: Poems.
Identifiers: Canadiana (print) 20210215992 | Canadiana (ebook) 20210216026 |
    ISBN 9781774220269 (softcover) | ISBN 9781774220276 (PDF) |
    ISBN 9781774220283 (HTML)
Classification: LCC PS8615.E785 C67 2021 | DDC C811/.6—dc23

ONTARIO ARTS COUNCIL
CONSEIL DES ARTS DE L'ONTARIO
an Ontario government agency
un organisme du gouvernement de l'Ontario

Gordon Hill Press gratefully acknowledges the support of the Ontario Arts Council.

Gordon Hill Press respectfully acknowledges the ancestral homelands of the Attawandaron, Anishinaabe, Haudenosaunee, and Métis Peoples, and recognizes that we are situated on Treaty 3 territory, the traditional territory of Mississaugas of the Credit First Nation.

Gordon Hill Press also recognizes and supports the diverse persons who make up its community, regardless of race, age, culture, ability, ethnicity, nationality, gender identity and expression, sexual orientation, marital status, religious affiliation, and socioeconomic status.

Gordon Hill Press
130 Dublin Street North
Guelph, Ontario, Canada
N1H 4N4
www.gordonhillpress.com

All the old thinking is about loss.
In this it resembles all the new thinking.

— Robert Hass

Language is a tool we use to inflect silence so we can hear it better.

— Li-Young Lee

Looking closely helps.

— Anne Carson

For My Father, Kevin William Heslop,
I make my love engrafted to this store:

Table of Contents

a thought, barefoot

slips

along a
painter's
tendon,

pools

at the risk.

Wrist.

one whole third of your life is spent **getting used to gravity**

the italian word for high waves doubles as the word for horses
something in the coastal imagination blent the curve of manes

with the force of the wind i suppose so floating south from salerno
to viro valentina in the sleeper   i see skeins of white-faced ponies

ceremonial in bells gallop across the silent bluegreen tyrrhenian   sea
children ample in music dreaming on the beaches no final revelation

when my son was a boy   his theatre teacher   a woman who'd spent
sixteen months tending stables in her twenties told his mother and me

                actors   are like teenagers   are like horses

                    capable of bucking the very sky
                but with the nervous system of a hummingbird

        she must have sensed we didn't know what to make of him
                    the turbulence of his septembers

i think of him how   in the bakery in naples last week   a woman
her hand clutching a crucifix of brackish olive wood on a thin chain

told me that god could call him back   no trace of discomfort in her eyes
and is the man singing in the next car conscious of the crack of lightning

            over the bay on dim summer nights when nothing sings
                except the residue of misspent afternoons

and god could call him back call it   pain is bread   call it
the universe is a rainstreaked bakery   call it   when he was in hospital

it wasn't me who asked for the semi-private room   his neighbour sang
every night to shepherd his dreaming   he was a studio musician

    trained in decades of french horn   a young man   still   they were
    unable to prevent the subdivision of his   cancer cells 64th notes

had been his nemesis professionally he joked   it was the way my son
would comfort us at 4am he would comfort us on a tuesday up nightsick

lift an intubated hand smiling around a nasal cannula   give thumbs up
the way any patient recited their diagnosis   the latin a colosseum falling

i see why dostoyevsky flung raskolnikov at the flaying that broke nietzsche
as waves of white horses buck in their breaking on the shore towards god

could speak she said   clutching his only son begotten in olive wood
               the word doubled   crucifix or caduceus

                    bluegreen turning   into waves

 fed to axioms   i fell upon the earth   and ran
to where   when   in the valley the colour comes

there is a deciduous solitude   the whorl
                                of the novel describes

as cloud   that philosopher   turns the earth
        in its hands tatters   muttering   One

full third of your life   is spent   getting used to gravity
        Son   fireflies in the forest   like opinions

take their metre from lovers   not Lethe
                        you are mistaken   Run

as light issues   perspective on collapse
              together i'm thinking   nu

-clear armageddon sounds the prettiest   the most tangential
                                        now
                        just
to protest evictions   tomorrow and tomorrow and this morning

in the rain   en masse   wielding   the social river
              all day   in the riot   in the rain

makes more   sense   than the former
                blur of   endeavour as   the con

-temporary surplus autopilot clusterfuck   edits
                                        a mere   boy

in the evening   when
              the one and only   weird   world   is   still

actually listening to ducks is preferable to the predicated pinprick religion

the virus is the thought we are individuals the thought we are individuals *is*
the virus   *is* the thought *we are* individuals the thought we are individuals *is*

the virus *is*   make the impermeable barrier of the self great a
-gain wealth forgetting all but   self i   have to tell you yes the thought

we are   individuals is   the virus i was   walking by the very geese
seem to have   i'm sure it's nothing serious but   forgotten how to migrate

standing like steer in the overhyped grass amidst the sort of snow build up

the river its referred countenance horizontal gravity ducks seem to prefer
sidelong pinnacle gymnastics of light on water turning like recall i was won

-dering about the manifested of it   meanwhile this radical white indivi-
dual inclined smallpox folk the western world must have longed for escape

to city hall the hill a pimple and taut white apex a static quo installed
as all get out   refusing to example we   i holiday want this   photo to be

absolutely massive involuntarily overwhelming towards the united states of
your contemplative grandmother sitting by the window   the stopgap elect

-ricity run down illustrious president bullshit wrought it's we or *none* of us
where has what the geese have forgotten gone   let's consider broadening

palette verbally   a little bit   seeing a little bit   past the us them
her him cis trans here there binary bullshit people the river is Washing-

ton on ton on ton on ton on ton on ton of polypropylene involuntarily
listen carefully claim to be individual   then breathe   you are   linked to

-gether with   forever is   in your   lungs when   you think
us them   when you   think us   them what   is   in are your lungs

please   call it spectacle   grand   or please   call it out-
    side sky art   chalk   it up   to   gather

appreciate   watching   together why
    does every   thing need to   be political abs-

olute extreme   move on   i prefer not to
    get beaten with your clandestine camera instead to call it out

  -side   emblematic   bread   and   circus   people   if
we   were   talking for a sec   sure   but you've noticed

the incrementally warmer world of the getting getting getting credit
card mixed with children sacrificed to an extreme Jesus Christ fetish

this several thousand kilometre an hour sneeze distancing planes
Northrop   Grumman   Lockheed   Martin   manufactured

does it look beautiful over institutionalized better together Canada

which isn't   as   the the art of the deal guy con
-tracts covid and a group of planes   whose business now is north-

wards of the stars   and the stripes   the eagle   and the good

time do we know which how many families in Afghanistan whose
killing dovetails   with our entertainment   what fiscally Ca-

nada contributed to that how many soldiers participated in that
do we find in that entertainment the belief that the luck of the draw

that institutionalized binary that Canada we talk about is better

to achieve balance   .   in the profoundly   cliff time we are
look at your cousin   in his digital echochamber   his terror there

ask an actual why   of the distillation   he feels he is   why is he

opposed in   space in a chaos of   trepidation that is   a grocery store
among the most   misunder-

stood on the planet no   orator no   oblivious of the white cis settler list

-ens institutionally suspicious   approaching   in the cliff time we are
what look like undercovers   cousin   is rudimentary liberty becoming

rhetorical   and   listening   he says he listens to the Peter-
son podcasts books the lectures   asked a girl out   told no   not dumb but

Christian confused frustrated overworked underpaid incapable of an act
-tual shooting but   in the cliff time we are   listen ask

an actual why   in the trepidation of the cliff   he is your cousin
that   is his terror there   he is your cousin

oh that's the universe in absolutely radically caps lock accordance with forever

—*for Réiltín*

in the masked static of our time the question of the edge is of precise diptych
of whether remote   chaos   without   order   is   possible   however

suspending in sanitizing gel the discrete infinities of language bubbles we are
disordered and ordered   the   crystalline   kin   we   are just now as one

community without impulse to you me my your us them viral binaries thin-
king English distinction requires as a syntax of sunlight in italics on the river

is a larger disordered more incomprehensible saying   remote from our chaos
but beautiful a protestor example sentence playing in the grizzly scree and we

six feet between us our complex   silent   yelling on the endless public-
ation while nature consciously criss-crossing themselves protests oblivious of

resolution disorienting grammar   like   love   consciously   trans

-piring the masked   infinites   we   are   can will go on forever here
so go to pot to a bottle go to Cleveland   you can't take the edge off a sphere

recontextualizing an end to 2001 where there is all this hay around
you will continue to see them   again and again

old contemporary and parallel   art science and technology
a better breadth of story   all the central human works past love

would you feel   if not for disaster   some semblance of duty
some nuclear holistic music   handed down   to document

forever possibly exists   to photograph   truth on its head
would you have doctored the forgotten   lighting the sky

morning ditty

—for Heather

the sun shines   on the air   and softens it
which breeze makes torquings in   as poems are

like grief   makes eddies human
                all too often

call it elegiac   but   Terribly Forlorn
listen to the aether   whisper

  volta volta   *volta*   *volta*   *volta*

a parliament of angles

because suburbia   is falling   i had to stand
at the intersection   and the artefact

off-camera   a cop explaining   recursion at great length
   to a gap   in the middle of the road

my body is an art of desperate   exclusion
                         framed suddenly

don't remind me   to tell you the story about the world
on the eve of the fiasco of souls   during the emblematic day

capitalism shot that Vermont state messenger appealing on the spot

through   and through
to   beauty in   beauty out   so   don't sugar-coat

the pulpit   the gas cult
                after   saying to the future   no

to pretty the organization of that which is soon to be known formerly as **hope**

observing how you went a few steps at a time to parchment:

a found poem in four acts for the disabled poem-making entity known as Roxanna Bennett
which bears this very went-to-school smart person subtitle you are reading now

i.

observing how you went a few steps at a time to parchment
to put things so endeavouring
to listen
to put the event of endeavouring description so pretty
to put observing sparrows trying delightful
to decide whether or not
the organization of hope
is poetry

ii.

is poetry
the organization of hope?
the suitably excessively wordy organization of hope a few steps at a time?

iii.

is poetry a got money to buy peanuts
i think so
i think i cannot reasonably fit squawking into the few steps at a time
making of myself
when you
endeavouring the hassle
to put body mind to quill
to pretty the organization of that which is soon to be known formerly as hope
to make the hope walk
like toddlers on a playground
a few at a time
squawking delightful
so excessively worthy of hope

iv.

so rest the food of rest
as i decide to thank you
to thank you and yours suitably
for whether or not the trying a few steps at a time to quill parchment
is soon to be
you are
whether or not the panic of the blues has its own ideas
you are
and when you are no longer
and i cannot be
the sparrows and the chipmunk and the four juvenile blue jays
squawk poetry
their beaks like toddlers
to thank you for making them able to try
to be

about the twice-bent blast of that good night

— *for Bradley Scott Heslop*

i.

Into the habitable painting of the world, a text
like *What's happening bro?* arrives. "Fuck,"

candidate responses start. "Fuck, I don't
know. What's happening with you?"

The world and everything in it. That night,
abacus was from the Hebrew word for dust;

calculus, a pebble, from the Latin.
"I know that it's a stupid question, but

how are you doing?"

ii.

Grief is a time zone without a calendar.
"But define dust." *Tiny particles of earth*

or waste matter on surfaces or carried in the air.
Into the world of a habitable painting, a text

is summoned to the ear as if by friction caused
by entering its colour. *Fuck* the text

of the world begins; *fuck* it concludes. Acrylic
runs from every dog's mouth on every side

–walk in every city in the world and hear,
brother, in every endless tongue, in every style

of union or revilement, the text of the world:
Fuck. I whisper to the windowsill, brother;

I draw my fingertip along the windowsill
and tell my fingertip's corona, *Brother.*

care-painted How are you? whispers at the well of collaborative thought

—for Síle of the Untypeably Lovely Name

Through the stormy quiet of my recent disconnect   She says hello
She says   I need at least to hear exactly what participating people do
I too would love to hear from the participating people   but more so
I would that you and Liz were spinning   feeling present   just in case
our time is only pretty updates   partial words   projects   reminders
a social interaction in a moment   quiet joys   a badly wanted feeling
the Supreme Court updates thinking.

some of the time I love feeling
the past is not sure just what a present is   exactly   and that she thinks
people think   now   is just the Supreme chant they prefer not to hear
She says hello? She says   I'm sorry   I've only just received responses
She says I would love but I'm not pretty feeling.   I hear updates and
I am interested in participating but more so I am feeling painted diff-
icult in recent time. I'm no longer partial. I'm exhausted/uncomfort-
able/uncertain and I would prefer the lovely poets just   disconnect
just

for

now
so I could send well-balanced words   spinning like turquoise teacups.

A truth is we hold memories too meaningful
to punish with the anecdotal telling of translation
into brittle words, as equally there are some memories
too sacred for review: the ilk of faces they contain,
held wrapt in neural silk, suspend above the storm
of harms the world can be, like a perfect eyelash
on a sleeping baby's cheek, untouchable
because of that concern that sleep would not return
after a wakening—so sleep, a little, memory: sleep.

there is no minor violence just as there is no negligible cough during an aria

Listen: someone's saying a prayer in a locked bathroom.
Someone's locked tongue jangles in prayer. Peculiar
this attempt to offer syllables as if to speak of her.
This mumbling under thunder. This candle lit
for that spectacle which ends not with a curtain falling,
but a thunderbolt from a cloudless sky.

        Oh, that the sky were cloudless.
There is no minor violence just as there is no negligible
cough during an aria. Visitors are welcomed to the school
of lost tongues. History, by changing its name, is the hero,
or heroine, of this story. I comb my mind for images
and find women from some millennium gone, their fingers
singing in berries (must have been) Etruscan cloth
hampered in the wind blowing violet wisps of their hair
gathered in the manner of their mothers, of their grand-
mothers, with brooches lifted from the land (must have been).
Just think! Not to be committed to any law of dissolution.
Consider the parlance of women battered as proverbs.
Listen: she is running into the rain, a swaddled nova
        in her arms; the screen door like a jaw snaps behind her.
Listen: she is weaving a prayer in her hands like a basket
        no crack of the tusk, voice of the angry man, shall touch.
Peculiar this attempt to ascribe brushstrokes to elephants.
Peculiar this star, this candleflame in the open sky at dusk.

In the flummoxed half-light of the bus, staring
vacantly at the stubbled shins of strangers—
when the desert becomes too much, I guess
mammals tend to lodge one knee into the sand
as the body sways and gives and this is why
femurs grow like wildflowers there; the addax
comes to mind—it was the way they would arrange
the plastic grocery bag on the felted blue seat,
a second by their feet in ballet flats which kicked
as if thoughtlessly trying to shake off that tattoo.
As of this afternoon, I can say that I've been bitten
by mosquitoes from two separate area codes
within a twelve-hour span. With that sentence,
I hoped to tell you how I felt—of particular relevance
is the first line break. Also the distances. We don't
plan these things, but this is how they come about.
Did I mention that the light was touching everything?

I write tonight as what remains of much
of Notre Dame is sunken, smouldering ash:

cathedrals can't keep morning light out.
To let the evening light return

and laughter govern gravity—
the vines we were at daybreak stir and ask

One minute more? Just one more, here?—
I'd have the earth stand still and sing

the sun forever fled.

I caught myself near dawn saying *Hey Siri*
in the bedfolds' halfdark reaching for—

and finding—

halfdark bedfolds only. Marinate a brain
in metaphors all night and meet a U-shaped

conference table of Apple's brand ambassadors—

all glass and dawn and brushed aluminum
and overlooking an improbably-named city

like Cupertino, California—

algorithming names. *Hey Siri, What's*
the universal language we invented but

which failed? Don't say love. The key
would be to find the essence of name

without the encumbrance of etymology
or class. It must both signify the elder

sister standing in a culturally indistinct kitchen—

she dries a plate whose golden inner ring
is splitting August evening's slanting through

the curtained window just above the sink.
Her brothers, mutable and patterning

as algorithms running by. She thinks
she'll drop the plate and clucks her tongue

loud enough to slow them down next time,
softly enough to land shy of a scolding—

and equally the Sanskrit-speaking royalty
bathing in milk somewhere formidable

and gone. *It has to be two syllables*
a man announces to the room that way

that men are wont to announce things to rooms—

linguistics PhD-turned-Ad Exec.

who tells himself he'll give it all up to translate
full-time again someday soon. *Two syllables*, he says

again. *Not three.* I asked Siri what the etymology
of her name was. *Siri is just the name they gave me*

when I got the job, she says. *It doesn't mean*
any one specific thing. But I like it.

Wikipedia says its Norwegian meaning is
beautiful woman who leads you to victory

and was fathered indirectly by a glut of US military
acronyms. The charm of *when I got the job.*

I'd woken from the dream in which a man,
who in the dream I both was and could see,

mutters Esperanto to himself and walks. Limestone
and moonlight. Mulled wine in a teal ceramic cup

in his hands. Cobblestones and somewhere
inexact. *Hey Siri, What is a chemise? What is a sari?*

A harpist's crinkled linen sweeping by embellishes
the cobblestones. Silken moonlight. Barefoot

in the dream, the harpist shows him the eczema
stippling—

Hey Siri, What is another phrase for the back
of your knees?—

as if entrusting him with a world. In the dream,
he touches them—

Popliteal fossa—

and then I wake, retrieve my hands, and find
my fingertips are daubed with someone's blood.

As a kid I had run up the stairs and slipped on the slick
of the landing into an awareness my body was not just
a means of exhilaration: I woke in stiff, starched sheets
with a careful plastic clothespin on my finger throbbing
synchronously with my skull, and a stranger explained
an adhesive was used "right here: it's just like the glue
you have at school, but this is stronger and for healing."
Afterwards, I remember feeling deeply disappointed
as if in this negligible way I had failed to demonstrate
any talent for self-destruction: I'd be unable to parade
the beautiful white cast which would magnetize the grace
of girls I was beginning to notice or offer at recess
the igneous stitchwork of another boy to inspection.
And so from my first foray into the storm of harms
the world can be, I emerged with a desire, with me still
to have broken.

There's a sappy syntax,
lover:

nothing's out of place.
Every image shares

in the languid, familiar burning
of the sky

alien vowels so instant
they shimmer. Ash:

scatter-brained, tense-changing,

rhythmically-awkward poem, Ash;
Ash, spectacles and leather jacket,

vivid lover, sweet poem, my cohesion.

And I'm sorry these are unfamiliar
terms, substituting

the disadvantage of the penultimate grasp
for something easier:

you've got a love poem;
I've got an internal function,

and I hope this affirms your sense
of we as rhymed.

Mellifluous is from the late
Latin for *runny honey*.

Mellifluous is from the late
Latin for *honey, running*.

When you left
you took
almost everything.

or what you called in one poem **the frail light of birches**

all the wrong ghosts live here

— *Co-written with Jenny Berkel and Síle Englert*

On one of his last evenings as himself, my brother
leads me through the fairgrounds: the older sibling's
job is to explain the fear of falling. He's seventeen,
we're both oblivious. It's always autumn in the dream

and months from now we'll find him vomiting tarantulas
into an empty bucket in his lap until he falls asleep.
It's autumn and the carnival is brambles, weedy pavement,
lustrous sky, the creak of white carousel horses cracking

in October sun; a finger of warmth inside the scratches
left behind. Bumper cars like ampersands guided by chance
and circumstance in a threadbare ballet. He holds
a strip of tickets like the keys to all salvation

and lurches towards a rusted, low-slung moon.
Across the empty thoroughfare, no barker summons
but his shadow burned in pinstripes on the ground
speaks for him, daring us to try our luck,

spin the wheel. Singing our future, the ghost of music
calls out a canticle in bells—the clink and jangle
clockwork of clanking gears. Sour piano strings stir still.
Somewhere tetrapods form and warp between mirrors

in the funhouse. All the wrong ghosts live here:
two tucked safe behind steel in the ferris wheel's cart
as the whinging round begins. Below, our world
grows microscopic; the sky pulls us up and away.

This gravity won't break us when we fall. My brother,
ecstatic, watches my face fracture in the pulsing
lights. In the dream it's always autumn and how
could we have known that everything would turn?

speak to me

— for Kevin William Heslop

How long a way you've walked, my friend, to come six feet.
How long, how long a way you've walked my friend.

You seem to me to be a walking autumn. Speak to me.
You seem to me to be a speaking happenstance I love.

And when, in the blent, tense air of our first meeting,

      in the long dew drop spinning
      in the knot of the foisted cane
      in the quiet of pianohammers
      in the rain

the correct fury of your why is a mountain.

"Let's say it was one of those windfall nights in July when four friends sit mostly sitting and not speaking around a campfire illuminating their faces in a pattern whose unpredictability, at that hour and depth of saturation, if the data could be harvested and charted, would show clusterpoints—that was term that came to mind—*trends* which would certainly reveal something about the implicit mathematics of the universe like the stars alternately concealed and disembarked from by clouds moving coldly like the tattered thoughts of the world not helping anyone just above their heads. The hour is the one with the curve in its back, booze in its belly, blood in its cheeks and one of the friends saying, almost involuntarily, in part revelation and part considered admission, that she wishes she had married someone who could play the piano. She is a lab technician, let's say, which means that earlier tonight she relieved her scalp of the gentle ache the bun of her hair makes and the campfire light in her loosed hair plays like young cats in the sand as the four friends mutually witness this unmolested true sentence she has just spoken hanging before them as the fire bites and crackles away at it and one of them says, *Mhmm*; and the four produce the laughs they are inclined or accustomed to do on such a windfall night in July. It's late, and human beings have met to suture the wounds the railroads have made across this country bled for centuries of ore and oil and timber and flesh and precious metals in a manner reported by the poor swollen news networks—miasmic with commercials selling the exhausting obligation of happiness—as a national railroad shut down. That was the phrase, *shut down. St. John's Newfoundland running low on propane in one of the coldest winters in its history* declares the italicized preface to an article commissioned by a media conglomerate funded, in large part, by the very oil corporation to which our prominent economists apply the verb haemorrhaging—as in the phrase *haemorrhaging capital*—unironically. And what would John the Apostle say of the matter except that propane had no business in his namesake to begin with? And what was propane? But—St. John fathoming propane—would you say we may have wandered from our subject? No one of the friends wants to say a word or shift their seat around the campfire for fear that it might precipitate thoughts of the morning and the children whose bellies they are responsible for settling with orange juice and eggs and toast into whose peanut-buttered surface a knife is drawn in the shape of a heart like the stencils we have made on cavewalls and gravestones for hundreds of thousands of years—a species preparing our little ones for the day stretching uncomprehending before them in the sun which shone, as Beckett would have it, upon the nothing new. What could children know of the provinces and jurisdictions we have devised criss-crossed with bulk freight they'd identify, parked before a train crossing, as *choo-choo's?* And how, in good conscience, to slip the paperback, perfect-bound workbook with the harmonious drawings of the eco-system into the glittering pink and blue Dora the Explorer backpack after the six-year-old has carefully nibbled around the edge of the heart drawn in the peanut butter so that the toast is the shape of a heart, her baby teeth having near-perfectly defined its edge? And what to do but lift this child and kiss her inconsolably? And when the bus pulls away from The Waving Place on the corner, what to do but return to the nook to pick up, with two fingers, the plastic cup she emptied of concentrated orange juice and the plate, stippled with crumbles and flecks of peanut butter, and bring them to the sink and convince your scalp into its professional bun and stand with your throat in your hands wondering what in the world is coming next?"

Like a just-spent flashbulb in its concave theatre tiring,
Czesław's mind incandesces, comforting the things
Of this tortured earth. When composing verses,
He abided by two virtues: diligence and resignation.
I dreamt I asked "What is the etymology of literature?"
And saw a smudge of mischief in his eye, replying
"Well, the word is of three parts: lit, terra, tour."
Miłosz was claimed by a Catholic crypt—*Bene Quiescas*—
And the page, equally supine, remains, dreaming,
Perhaps in chalk, of thistles, of dragonflies.

I don't know what's on the other side of that pine fence
but whatever it is it is my neighbour

the centuries like stumps in a storm concede nothing

the difference between the glacialweight of a lockjaw solitude
and a tender sociability has something to do with steam irons

crippled van goghs begging nickels of shined shoes of the city millipede, hustling

a poem is a cluster of nerves, borrowed
fingertip, damp beach

they gave him a hero's welcome. which is to say
they said nothing of his inevitable decline

like teflon emptied of sirloins and just
the smeared fat beads reminiscing, these modern syllables struggle to mean

what privilege it is to now read nothing poems

I go, you stay, two moons

waiting in line at the supermarket, all this broken beef
in all this supermarket line at the beef, broken
all this line at the supermarket this line in
the supermarket all this broken beef, waiting

"Which was when we met the guy who said he was a 'body artist'—do you remember? 'Artista del corpo.' That he considered his body, which he built methodically from moment to moment, the canvas—he used a word which more closely translates as the 'arena'—of his work. Which I thought was horseshit: the bundle of endorsements he received from a supplement manufacturer in Milan allowed him to eat very well and work out twice a day and add to an indisputable physique the convenient artist imprimatur in his involved self-advertisement to the opposite sex. He was beautiful, but the proportions of his art had been arranged in advance; and this freed him from producing a statement of aesthetics, which is what (I thought) artists are obligated to do. I was suspicious and told you so when we finally got away for lunch on the balcony overlooking the square in Lamezia. 'I prefer statues which don't draw breath,' I had said. 'Call me old-fashioned if you will.' Scoffing, you had identified his artistry of the body, of the breath, of the will to self-actualize the instrument with which we perform the kinetic aria of our lives, as an almost religious vocation; I admitted he was gorgeous. You sneered, asking what the Buddhist monks were doing when they sounded the bell to initiate morning prayer and sat down in full lotus to balance their limbs 'in such a way as to focus—the breath, the heartbeat—on unrippling the pond of consciousness.' 'Consciousness?' I asked. 'No restriction, then, on who can be an artist? Shouldn't time and evolution have been judicious in their liberation of individual bodies to self-select as artists simply for being what they are?' 'But how many people have you heard claim body artistry?' you asked, forcing cessation. Because after all we were sitting on a balcony in Italy overlooking the smoked limestone of an ancient square dotted with white parasols shading carts of produce brought to the square before sunrise. 'Look at the clouds just being,' you said. 'Look at the blue of the sea in its pact with the horizon and the sky where tufts of cloud suspend—taking in the view—disinterested in debate about the legitimacy of any one form of artistry. Look at them being what they are without this endless accordion of thought or justification.' 'You are a cloud,' I told you adoringly. 'I am and you are too,' you said, which was when the plate of steamed mussels in the white wine brio arrived on a brief Italian sonata spoken by the waiter whom I didn't understand precisely—your Italian had surpassed mine that summer—and we had both said *Grazie* and I leaned back into my Campari and spread, on a wafer of baguette, the olive oil-doused bruschetta I was crazy about and would later fail to replicate—'It was the tomatoes,' you would say—and I thought of the body artist, beginning to forgive him. Thinking that, perhaps, bidden as our bodies are into this forceful ballet of chance and suffering, perhaps this cultivation of one's own vessel, sole coil, mobile prison, et cetera was in fact an act of resistance to the unrequested life through which we hasten—as Nabokov would have it—at some forty-five hundred heartbeats per hour towards the grave. Why not, I thought to myself, let the sculpting of each moment accrete into the spiraled aspiration of the body? Why not—I was thinking of the controlled motion of the interpretive dancer I had admired back home—let the body remind us that the world consists of atoms and emptiness and we are the little parts of it with agency? You had seen, then, my face detach from itself and you said, smiling your smile, lifting an imperfect mussel out of its steam-canted shell with a small bifurcated fork catching the summer sun, 'You're doing it again.'"

A midnight sky is starless and its new moon is a paring.
No: the last sheet of black construction paper in the stack
of 29 the first-grade teacher didn't press the punch quite
through has three partial holes. Shine a high-watt flashlight
from behind the uppermost of them. *There's* your slivered moon.
The inquiry is whether we considered that the bleaching sun
would rub the stain from flags and abrogate pro patria.
It did: from weird, lunar trees time would have white flags
like twisted linen hang like pendulums like cab drivers. Tonight,
take a little comfort in the knowledge that the rub of time
will launder from the earth our every justified trespass.

this is not an elegy because the world is full of elegies and i am tired of consoling and being consoled

i.

"During the pandemic, I learned we yearn to witness human behaviour most, perhaps, when relieved of the exhausting obligations of speaking and behaving in the neurochemical flush accidents of eye-contact and permutations of performance compel in the place, formerly known as public, where one endeavours to order a cup of coffee. And amid the old blear slant of light angling through the window at dawn, I learned that the impulse to apply deodorant is a will to alienation even as the cosmic stupor of lit dust churning by the sill takes it upon itself to tell us what we're meant to do to be together here and we—desperate for but oblivious to the how of it—smear that wet duck's feather-tuft of hair with incorporated scent. Like the woman to whom I read these words first: she is lifting her arms to vector light, peach-coloured linen over auburn hair and her supple bareness until she sees, and wrinkles her nose in mock offence at, you. (There's a line of Earle Birney's asking to be spoken: 'With dusk I am caught / peering over the holly / hedge at the dogwood.') A grad student of sociology, she walks barefoot across the sunlit hardwood of her comfortable village loft to lift the kettle for chamomile with a drop of ethical honey. Thinking of how the gazes which crosshatch public places affect women's awareness of their personal bodies—a dog soliloquizes birds shimmering upwards from the neighbour's backyard's maple tree into the endless overcast overhead—with particular focus on the shift in perception among women wearing, or not wearing, a brassiere. *Such that a positive consequence of this pandemic*, she is thinking, tilting the kettle over the mugs, *consists in the radical reduction in the number of breasts subject to unwelcome scrutiny in public places*. A train is passing by and the sound it makes is not consistent. *Sounds*, she thinks. *Plural*. Like what, after lighting beeswax candles and turning off the fan-connected bathroom light last night, the hot-water-filled bathtub invokes—*Resonant plurality*, she thinks—providing the same improving element to the speaker of poems that the shower provides, for whatever reason, to the singer of songs. ('Of course,' Hass is saying, 'we stand to reason and lie down to dream.')"

ii.

"The poems in question, Henrik Norbrant's *When We Leave Each Other*—sent across all the air over the Atlantic by my second cousin Karen, an historian and teacher in Copenhagen—had been translated from the Danish to pour out 'clear, cold, and mineral-tanged as spring water.' When we met some summers ago in Montréal, I'd asked her husband about his countrymen's inductive tradition of deer hunting in a dialect self-satisfied with the reading I had been doing as an undergraduate: 'Shouldn't one question the morality of hunting from a position of abundance rather than one of necessity?' And he had replied, 'If you don't ask such questions of yourself, you shouldn't hunt' with a directness and candour that made me long to be inducted into adulthood in that country I haven't seen and fear I may never. Earlier that day, Karen asked what foods I preferred for breakfast. 'Coffee, eggs, bacon, toast.' 'Ah, that sort of thing,' she replied, unable to hide her disappointment in youth flung irretrievably from the hygge-bosom of Scandinavian influence into the flabby, blotched arms of late-capitalist-settler fare. Karen, I write to you now to say I've learned of our many unobtrusive cereals, of the jams and rolls and of the cheeses, of the yogurt stippled with muesli, too late. I sit, indolent and biddable, before a laptop, following the endless issuance of morbid witticism characteristic of the millennial underclass on Twitter as we wonder what our leaders have in store. I hope you and Peter are well. I like to think of the two of you walking the cobblestones of Nørrebro, arm in arm, talking about all there is to know; it calms me down, a little, to think of you. On this side, we are gorging on stories of love, hope, and remorse in the endtimes as seen on Netflix, our fingers seeking those of our lovers in the textured dark. The culture here is irretrievably doused in oil and beliefs whose course, until fire is finally upon it, with flames to our very doors, none of us notices, like the protest of Buddhists a half century past, you'll remember, sitting in public like lotuses, their tangerine robes darkened and heavy with petrol, waiting for the light."

fragments of amber in the grass dewy their whole life long

Listen, you said turning suddenly at the gate.
This place is sacred to me. Don't fuck it up.

Ben and that sax bent like a candle to its food
brings Icarus to envy for not singing falling.

Poetry is philosophy in evening-wear.

Some
assemb
lyreq
 u, i, red.

There's something comforting about a nearby electric fan
whirling towards and into oblivion and back out again.

The Tweet Shall Inherit the Verse.

Fly; window; disbelief.

Idleness causes gossip as still water causes mosquitoes.

isn't the only substance
whose shape is determined
by the instrument
with which
it is
cut.

conversations on going

Here is where the woman made of rhythm drinks.
Anastasia cues a Chopin nocturne from her early years
when grace and prodigy and national endowments
flung her into something second cousins still recall
with quiet pride at home in Volgograd, in Saratov.
"Very simple," she explains to her new students
who have lingered lithely after evening lessons ended.
"Do not show when you are watching me."
Gym bags at their hips, ribboned pointe shoes
dangling from their shoulders, most of them leave
with quiet words or cigarettes; two students sit
in darkened quiet as from the stage's left wing, Anastasia,
in her helmet of zinc wire, begins describing running.

When David Foster Wallace said
fiction's about what it is

to be a fucking human being,
he didn't mean to insinuate

coitus is the principal occupation
of the imagination, but may have:

narrative, after all, loves the twilit
entanglement as much as anyone,

and the way the votive gyroscope
of two moving minds compresses

into the white-sheeted ordeal of a book
is, like the undaunted stain of lilac

later pressed between its pages, finally
sensual in nature and in name.

All talk is barren trade.
A writing on the wind's wall.

— Joseph Brodsky

i haven't seen the best minds of my generation anywhere

> lend
> me
> a
> lens

what does the cardinal mean when he
darts into the bush that way so   red

or   touching minds at table

the poem would break   as pears on the grass
and the low-flying bees who hunger   who listen

crowds
beget
crowd
thinking

Like a bead of blood on taut twine, my body
this ancient cabinet, can no longer make sense
of sound nor scent nor voice beyond my door.

if i sed   5'11"/225/75 yrs/56
books uv poems

if i sed   the latest of which is titled 'ths is erth, thees ar peopul'
that the painting on the cover was his

if i sed   2 hrs at 754 dundas st.

if i sed   shoulder length grey hair twiggy a cocked ball cap
green with yellow mesh, spectacles beneath the brim the bulbous nose
black t-shirt and a paunch, blue jeans' belt tight, shaggy loafers

if i sed   the kind of man you'd hate to see your daughter with (you thought)
bad knees, back an overlapping knots
a lilting voice in speaking, baritone in song

if i sed   xcellent

if i sed   he sed "i wuz told the salmon talks have been moved to early next week.
and i sed at least the salmon are talking!"

if i sed   he concluded his set with a stomping chant

if i sed   that the chant was "is it time to leave the hotel yet?"

if i sed   that between songs
some people were talking about what he was and what he wasn't
and one had declaimed in that way that constricts a café
he was a "performer!"
and that from the stage he said "you think?" and chuckled

if i sed   the café's door swiveled in inches and the winter wind
as the percussion and piano and bill reading and singing
that the chime of the bell over the door seemed to want to join in
or that he and the wind were joined then somewhere over the door

if i sed   he was holding two white sheets of printer-paper stapled
and he holding them
that shaggy big man who   if down the aisle your adult daughter

identified him as hers at the supermarket
when you ran into her incidentally might cause you to say
without having spoken to him "i'm ordering chinese for dinner;
come over tonight; it'll be just us two;
i feel like i haven't seen you in ages" he
reading a poem about a past lover
a poem written with his knuckles and throat
he holding them with one hand the two sheets with the poems

if i sed   a bird sensing gentleness settled there to permit him
to read from its wings

if i sed   some know that we love and some love that we know
that he would identify with the former and love the latter the same

if i sed   to give you a sense it was an animal in motion without the vicious
it was a sense of motion, an animal with the giving
and like any honest mortal performing
it was full of the past tense already

if i sed   it was long in the brevity and brief in the long
a meaning motion then
without the vicious an animal giving in the past tense already
performing in the brevity in the long

i sed   to give you a sense   it was

This morning I listen to a reading of Robert Hass's impromptu poem from a September night in Waterloo Village, New Jersey, beneath the pull, sway, and simmer of my backyard's maple tree, tweezing loose hairs from the arms of the keys of my sterling typewriter, itself an American product of enduring manufacture. It was issued, so to speak, like Hass, in 1941, a time, a social world when malteds were coming into vogue on the main streets of smalltown America—you'd see a family of four in a green Packard, top down, pulling in to park before the ice cream parlour's sidewalk's swarming with boys in checked shirts and pomaded hair and clutching the promise of a little hardwon pocket-money in their neighbour-loving fists, their sisters with blue or green or yellow ribbons in their hair, dresses blowing in the cooling but still humid twilight of that spent day—as Smith-Corona was beginning to assemble the first of the quarter million M1903A3 Springfield rifles they would produce during the Second World War. "Though the US military doesn't count—" recites Hass, "why put a weapon in the hands of your enemies?—by conservative reckoning, 9 500 Iraqi civilians were killed during the invasion of Iraq. By conservative reckoning, 300 000 Iraqi civilians have been killed during the occupation of Iraq." A bright-green key helicopters down from the maple in the interstices of whose movement, if you half-close your eyes, an enormous chandelier sparkles, turning. "Two and a half million Iraqis have been driven from their homes and are living in exile. Two million Iraqis, having been driven from their homes by ethnic cleansing, are living in internal exile. Last night, on television, a candidate for the presidency of this country described the state of affairs as 'winning.'" In the singsong voice and grammatical imprecision I affect when I speak to my five-year-old yellow lab, I tell him, as he heaves after having too quickly gobbled six scoops of red watermelon dropped on the tile at our feet as water was boiling on the stove for green tea, I tell him, "Hang on, puppy. I'll get you some good cold water because what else is there?" Thinking of how, in 1939, two years before Hass and that typewriter were produced, a Japanese scientist in Yokohama, Japan, invented the first seedless watermelons by producing a triploid hybrid—a technique that would come to be improved upon and patented by a Californian and lead to the obsolescence of the old American wives' tale that watermelon seeds, implanted in the stomach, would grow. And it was one year before that that Orson Welles and H.G. Wells gave their infamous CBS performance of *The War of The Worlds* from San Antonio, Texas. Nearly 120 000 Japanese Americans would be forcibly relocated over the course of the Second World War, following upon what H.G. Wells called the war to end all wars. But our concern is not, has never been, with the past: as I walk outside with the broad clear bowl of water slopping from lip to lip, I'm astounded by the number of houseflies who each morning and every afternoon appear about the screen door to the backyard's porch and overgrowth of green life with plaintive little supplications. Part of me thinks that, if they could, they would be praying, each fly about the length of your thumbnail bumbling against the still-unfamiliar net of which their tentative consciousness assures them, again and again. "Walt Whitman," Hass is asking, "Where are you?" The following applause comes from the hands and throats of an audience at a poetry festival which, had it assembled forty years earlier, might well have been characterized as red, its members tracked. I reach back to open the screen door and most of the flies get caught between the screen and its now-adjacent pane of glass, so I slide the door back and forth on its dry track, back and forth, until the last fly tumbles into the freedom it has been permitted. "Elizabeth Cady Stanton, Emma Goldman, Rosa Parks," recites Hass, "Henry David Thoreau. Where are you?" I return again to the typewriter to tweeze the last hairs made to seem to symbolize a kind of longing in the breeze between the concave pedestals on which the Roman alphabet lies in ready repose. And already two more flies are caught behind the screen. "Where do they keep coming from?" I wonder. They won't say "No."

In two good hands, cradle an acre aloft. Then shake the home soil free.[1]
This is what the floor stands on: "My celia, a philotrophic palimpsest,[2]

---

[1]   Thank You, Mom, Home Soil, First Reader, Lisa Kathleen, Doc, Wisdom-Teacher, Compassion-Well Unending, with all my Love & Admiration.

[2]   Thank You, Dad, Home Base, Moral Imperative, Kevin William, Captain, Integrity-Teacher, "The Best We've Got", Night Sky, with all my Love & Respect. I'll see your name in lights.

circumferential epigenesis,   substrate capillary network, fungal fabric,[3]
dendrite-carpet, diachronic tapestry, my celia;   my celia, immaculate[4]

3   Thank You, Bradley Scott the Vast-Hearted & Mark Daniel the Beautiful, Brother-Tax Triumvirate Perpetual: I couldn't imagine better right hands.

4   Thank You, Gramma Heslop, Resilience-Teacher & Thank you, Grandpa Heslop, Fortitude-Teacher; Thank You, Gramma Stub, Patience-Teacher & Thank You, Grandpa Stub, Dignity-Teacher.

dispersive,   giant's cat's cradle'd relational symphonic, intransicranial,[5]
timid and timorous as bells, my celia;   my celia, photoresponsive weft,[6]

---

5   Thank-You to All My Relations, Human & Other, including the Trees taken
to mark these pages, here unnamed but stewarded in my every alveolus, my every blood
cell, my every shifting, humourless molecule …

6   Thank-You to the Teachers (appreciating "Mrs" is [sic], that two of you failed
me in English class & in chrono. order): Mrs. Hill, Mrs. Willer, Mrs. Hawkins, Mrs.
Strong, Mr. McCarthy, Mr. Moore, Mrs. Oliver, Mrs. Cousins, Ms. Goyette, Brenden
Douglas, Mrs. Sheppard, Ms. Beeler, Ms. Putnam, Rob LaRose, Mr. Evans, Mr. Spratt,
Mr. Needles, Mr. Chaudry, Ms. Palmer, Mr. Dundas, Ms. Miles, Marilyn Sweetland,
Rob Bell, John Leonard, Joel Faflak, Kate Stanley, Larry Garber, George Donaldson,
Madeline Bassnett, Ian Watson, Margaret Rossiter, Deshkan Ziibi, Nichiren Daishonin
& …

umbraresponsive warp, my celia; my celia, facilitant concernèd, webbed[7]
symbiogenesis blinking bifurcative through   the dew damp chronicle[8]

---

7   Thank-You to the Local Luminaries: Jennifer Chesnut, Tom Cull, Pam
Hannington, Tim Kelly, Josh Lambier, Miriam Love, Sandra De Salvo, Jenna Rose
Sands, Uncle Greg Stub, John Swales, Dennis White-Eye, Kate Wiggins; the Ineluctable
Friends: Wave/Photon/The Disabled Poem-Making Entity Known As Roxanna
Bennett, Derek Boswell, Vanessa Brown, Aidan Clark, Jack Copland, Jason Dickson,
Justin Dickson, Síle of the Untypeably Lovely Name, Peter Francis, P. Fraxineus Tego,
Shelly Harder, Colin Henderson, Liz Merwin, John Nyman, Jonathan Rath, Réiltín,
Aaron Schneider (whose idea the form of this poem was), and Phil Spina; the
Indispensible Workshop Peers & Friends in the Work: Jenny Berkel, Anita Bidinosti,
Conyer Clayton, Nicole Coenen, Jérôme Conquy, Ruth Douthwright, Síle Englert,
Camille Intson, David Janzen, Karen Louise, Erica "The Novelist" McKeen,
Dorit Osher, Tina Marion Rose, Jenna Rose Sands, Aaron Schneider, Kevin Shaw,
SOTULN[14], Kaitlin Torrance, and Andy Verboom.

8   Thank-You to Jeremy Luke Hill and Shane Neilson for their fortunately
payforwardable Work & Care and to the Editors, Publishers, and Jurists who have
given their Labour & Attention to the work in this collection previously appearing with
Anstruther Press, The Blasted Tree Art Collective and Publishing Company, *The Blue
Nib,* Collusion Books, *The Fiddlehead,* Frog Hollow Press, *ISACOUSTIC,* is/let, McIntosh
Gallery, *Juniper, Long Con Magazine, NOON: Journal of the Short Poem,* No Press, *Occasus Literary
Journal, One Sentence Poems,* Poetry London, Puddles of Sky Press, *talking about strawberries all of
the time,* TAP: Centre for Creativity, and *The Quarantine Review.*

of All This Not; my celia,   neuroplastic supradermal mesh tentacular;[9]
my celia, discursive forgetting filamentous,   (sub)terranean infinity...[10]

9   Thank-You to the Poets, who move(d) me, in brief: Jordan Abel, Dante Alighieri, Maya Angelou, Sacha Archer, James Arthur, John Ashbery, W.H. Auden, Elizabeth Bachinsky, James Baldwin, Amiri Baraka, David Barrick, Gary Barwin, Matsuo Basho, Madeline Bassnett, Charles Baudelaire, Dominique Béchard, Samuel Beckett, Billy-Ray Belcourt, Saul Bellow, Diana Beresford-Kroger, Wendell Berry, John Berryman, The Disabled Poem-Making Entity Known as Roxanna Bennett, John Betjeman, Earle Birney, Elizabeth Bishop, bill bissett, Dionne Brand, Joseph Brodsky, Julie Bruck, William Burroughs, Charles Bukowski, Yosa Buson, Italo Calvino, Albert Camus, Truman Capote, Anne Carson, Gaius Valerius Catullus, C.P. Cavafy, Mike Chaulk, Ta-Nehisi Coates, John M. Coetzee, Samuel Taylor Coleridge, Hart Crane, Michael Crummey, Phillip Crymble, Tom Cull, e.e. cummings, Kayla Czaga, HD, Mahmoud Darwish, Jack Davis, Jaclyn Desforges, Christopher Dewdney, Emily Dickinson, John Donne, Frederick Douglass, Robert Duncan, T.S. Eliot, Ralph Waldo Emerson, Sîle Englert, William Faulkner, Michael Fraser, James Fenton, Paola Ferrante, Ally Fleming, Carolyn Forché, Robert Frost, Jack Gilbert, Allen Ginsberg, Ulrikka S. Gernes, Laurie Graham, Günter Grass, Robert Graves, Sky Dancer Louise Bernice Halfe, Knut Pedersen Hamsun, Shelly Harder, Thomas Hardy, Robert Hass, Luke Hathaway, Seamus Heaney, Ernest Hemingway, Geoffrey Hill, Jeremy Luke Hill, Langston Hughes, Gerard Manley Hopkins, Karen Houle, Ted Hughes, Hồ Xuân Hu'o'ng, Kobayashi Issa, Randall Jarrell, Robinson Jeffers, Jim Johnstone, John Keats, Jack Kerouac, Thomas King, Galway Kinnell, Kirby, A.M. Klein, Patrick Lane, M. Travis Lane, Phillip Larkin, D.H. Lawrence, Li-Young Lee, D.A. Lockhart, Robert Lowell, Canisia Lubrin, Archibald MacLeish, Lee Maracle, Cormac McCarthy, Mary di Michele, Edna St. Vincent Millay, Khashayar Mohammadi, Toni Morrison, Czesław Miłosz, John Milton, Eugenio Montale, Marianne Moore, Andrew Motion, Sachiko Murakami, Vladimir Nabokov, Ogden Nash, Pablo Neruda, Shane Neilson, Henrik Nordbrandt, Alden Nowlan, John Nyman, Frank O'Hara, Adam O'Riordan, Wilfred Owen, Arleen Paré, Dominik Parisien, M. NourbeSe Philip, Sylvia Plath, Ezra Pound, Richard Powers, Jalal ad-Din Mohammad Rumi, Al Purdy, Shane Rhodes, Adrienne Rich, Rainer Maria Rilke, Ben Robinson, Shaun Robinson, Christina Rossetti, Muriel Rukeyser, Carl Sandburg, William Shakespeare, Kevin Shaw, Kenneth Sherman, Leanne Betasamosake Simpson, Gary Snyder, Stephen Spender, Gertrude Stein, John Steinbeck, Wallace Stevens, Mark Strand, May Swenson, Sappho, Aaron Schneider, Bardia Sinaee, Candace de Taeye, Kyoshi Takahama, John Terpstra, Souvankham Thammavongsa, Dylan Thomas, Hugh Thomas, Hunter S. Thompson, John Thompson, Tomas Tranströmer, Andy Verboom, Justin Vernon, Fred Wah, Derek Walcott, David Foster Wallace, John Wall-Barger, Robin Wall Kimmerer, W.B. Yeats, David White, Joshua Whitehead, Walt Whitman, Oscar Wilde, William Carlos Williams, August Wilson, Brandon Wint, Catriona Wright, Chuqiao Yang, & ...

10   & Thank-You, Dear Reader, for your Time, Tenacity & Good Taste.

Kevin Andrew Heslop wrote *con/tig/u/us* (The Blasted Tree, 2018), *there is no minor violence just as there is no negligible cough during an aria* (Frog Hollow Press, 2019), and *Human Beings Have Met to Suture the Wounds the Railroads Have Made Across This Country* (Anstruther Press, 2020); directed *Movements* (Museum London, 2021); and curated *six feet | between us* (McIntosh Gallery, 2022) where Deshkan Ziibi antlers through London Township Treaty (1796) territory. This is his first book.